A TRUE BOOK™

Women's History in the U.S.

The
FOUNDING
MOTHERS
of the
United States

Selene Castrovilla

Children's Press®
An Imprint of Scholastic Inc.

Content Consultant
Holly Hynson, MA
Department of History
University of Maryland, College Park

Thank you to Elise McMullen-Ciotti for her insights into Indigenous Peoples' history and culture.

A CIP catalog record of this book is available from the Library of Congress.
ISBN 978-0-531-13079-7 (library binding) 978-0-531-13338-5 (paperback)

All rights reserved. Published in 2021 by Children's Press, an imprint of Scholastic Inc.
Printed in North Mankato, MN, USA 113

SCHOLASTIC, CHILDREN'S PRESS, A TRUE BOOK™, and associated logos are trademarks and/or registered trademarks of Scholastic Inc.

Scholastic Inc., 557 Broadway, New York, NY 10012

1 2 3 4 5 6 7 8 9 10 R 30 29 28 27 26 25 24 23 22 21

Book produced by 22 MEDIAWORKS, INC.
Book design by Amelia Leon / Fabia Wargin Design

Front cover: (clockwise from top left) Phillis Wheatley, Mercy Otis Warren, Nanyehi/Nancy Ward, Martha Washington
Back cover: In 1782, Deborah Sampson dressed as a man and enlisted in the Continental Army.

Find the Truth

Everything you are about to read is true *except* for one of the sentences on this page.

Which one is **TRUE**?

T or F All Indigenous women sided with the British during the Revolutionary War.

T or F Women traveled to Revolutionary War soldiers' encampments to offer support and nursing care.

Find the answers in this book.

Contents

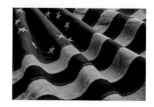

Penelope Barker

The **BIG** Truth

The Edenton Tea Party

Molly Pitcher

Women in a Turbulent Time

Before the United States was a country, it consisted of 13 colonies ruled by Great Britain, a nation that included England and Scotland, across the Atlantic Ocean. **Many colonists grew unhappy with taxes** the British king imposed without allowing them to participate in the government. Calling themselves **patriots,** these colonists began protesting **taxation without representation.**

One of the most significant **tax protests** became known as the Boston Tea Party. When the king put a tax on tea, it became very expensive.

On the night of December 16, 1773, about **70 patriot men** who tried to disguise themselves as Indigenous people dumped 342 chests of British tea into Boston Harbor. This act helped energize the patriots' cause. The colonists decided to organize and debate what actions to take against Great Britain. **Representatives** from each colony gathered in Philadelphia for meetings called the Continental Congress, which declared the colonies' **independence** on July 4, 1776. The American Revolution had begun!

Although women did not participate in the Boston Tea Party, they helped plan it.

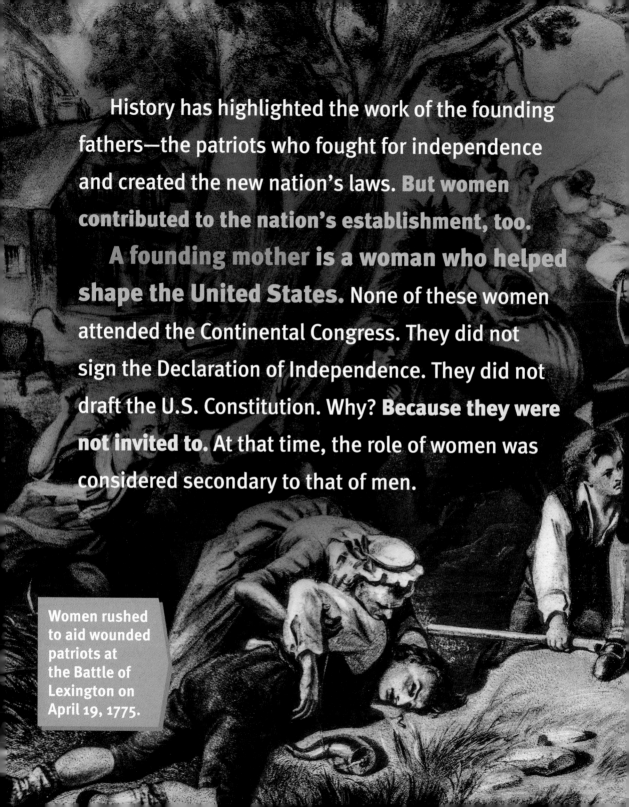

History has highlighted the work of the founding fathers—the patriots who fought for independence and created the new nation's laws. **But women contributed to the nation's establishment, too.**

A founding mother is a woman who helped shape the United States. None of these women attended the Continental Congress. They did not sign the Declaration of Independence. They did not draft the U.S. Constitution. Why? **Because they were not invited to.** At that time, the role of women was considered secondary to that of men.

Women rushed to aid wounded patriots at the Battle of Lexington on April 19, 1775.

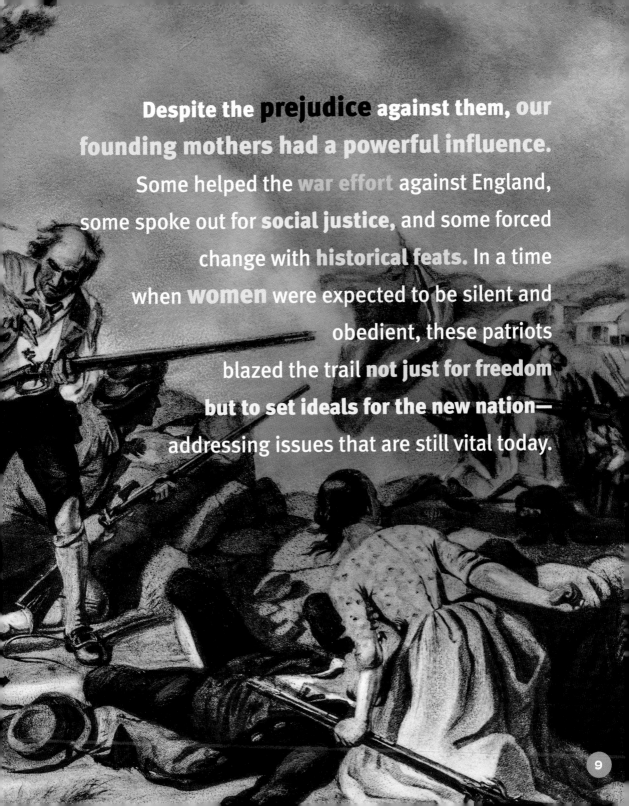

Despite the **prejudice** against them, our founding mothers had a powerful influence. Some helped the war effort against England, some spoke out for **social justice,** and some forced change with **historical feats.** In a time when **women** were expected to be silent and obedient, these patriots blazed the trail **not just for freedom but to set ideals for the new nation—** addressing issues that are still vital today.

Mercy Otis Warren

Revolutionary Writer

Mercy Otis Warren was a woman whose words urged the colonists to support independence. She was born in Barnstable, Massachusetts, on September 14, 1728.

Though the American Revolution wouldn't happen for almost 50 years, some citizens were against British rule even then. Mercy's father, Colonel James Otis Sr., was one of them. Mercy listened carefully to her father's revolutionary ideas. She agreed with his desire to live in a nation that was not bound by the laws of a government an ocean away.

When Mercy Otis was 26 years old, she married James Warren. They moved to Plymouth, Massachusetts, and had five sons. As revolutionary thoughts rooted in the colonies, Warren wanted to help them grow. Her husband was a **politician,** but she wasn't sure how she could help. Women did not hold positions of power and influence in the government at that time.

Mercy Warren was later known as the "Conscience of the American Revolution."

Sowing Seeds

Mercy decided she would **sow** patriotism in the colonies with words. She wrote and published satires about British colonial leaders—plays making fun of them. She published this work anonymously so she did not get into trouble with the government. Colonists read Mercy's plays and began to support the idea of revolution.

She continued to publish throughout the war and afterward, securing her place as one of our most inspiring and influential founders.

A statue of Mercy Otis Warren in Massachusetts, perhaps holding her 1790 book *Poems, Dramatic and Miscellaneous.*

Revolutionary Works

Mercy Otis Warren was the country's first female playwright. Three political plays she anonymously published between 1772 and 1775 helped ignite the revolution. Many patriots appreciated her influence. The second president of the United States, John Adams, wrote that God had given Mercy Otis Warren "Powers for the good of the World." In 1790, Warren finally dared to publish her name on a book of political poems and plays. In 1805, she released her final work, *History of the Rise, Progress, and Termination of the American Revolution,* a history of the American Revolution.

Phillis Wheatley

Enslaved Poet

Phillis Wheatley was born in West Africa around 1753. When she was about seven years old, she was **abducted** by slave traders and forced aboard a ship to America. She was sold to a man who bought Phillis as a servant for his wife.

Enslaved in Boston, Massachusetts, Phillis was very smart. Her owner decided to educate her. This was rare. Most slaves suffered under harsh conditions and were not allowed to learn to read or write.

When Phillis was 13, she began to write poems. Her first published poem appeared in a Boston newspaper on December 21, 1767. Many people did not believe an enslaved person, especially a woman, could create poetry.

In 1773, Phillis sailed with her owner's son to England, where a book of her poetry was published. Phillis was the first person of African descent, the first enslaved person, and the third female colonist to publish poetry.

Phillis's American name came from the ship, the *Phillis,* that carried her to America.

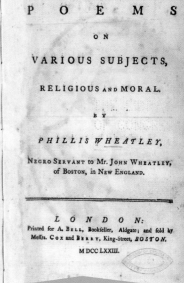

Freedom

Shortly after her book's release and her return to Boston, Wheatley was given her freedom. Meanwhile, colonists prepared to revolt against England. Wheatley supported the American Revolution. She wrote a poem celebrating George Washington's selection as army commander and sent it to him. He wrote back to her, thanking her. But she also believed that the issue of slavery prevented the colonists from achieving true heroism.

Poems on Various Subjects, Religious and Moral included Phillis Wheatley's portrait to prove she had written it.

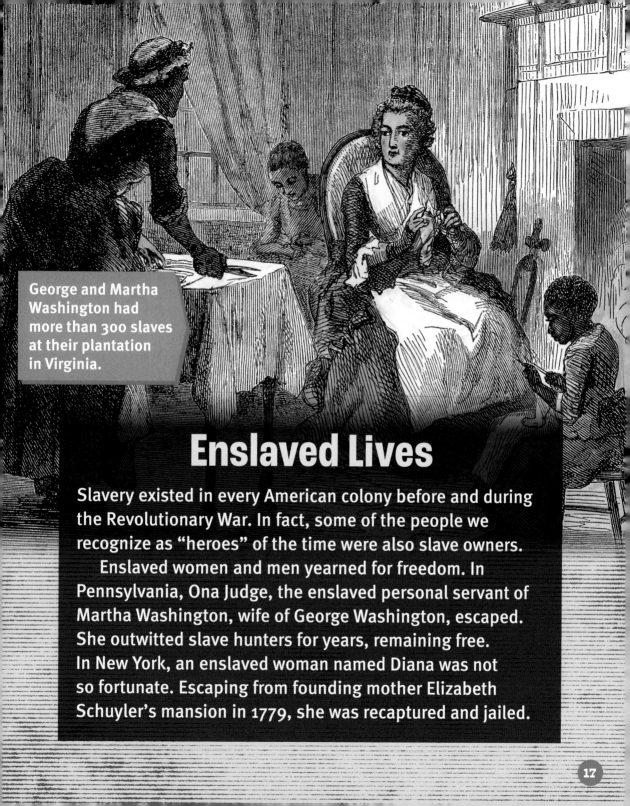

George and Martha Washington had more than 300 slaves at their plantation in Virginia.

Enslaved Lives

Slavery existed in every American colony before and during the Revolutionary War. In fact, some of the people we recognize as "heroes" of the time were also slave owners.

Enslaved women and men yearned for freedom. In Pennsylvania, Ona Judge, the enslaved personal servant of Martha Washington, wife of George Washington, escaped. She outwitted slave hunters for years, remaining free. In New York, an enslaved woman named Diana was not so fortunate. Escaping from founding mother Elizabeth Schuyler's mansion in 1779, she was recaptured and jailed.

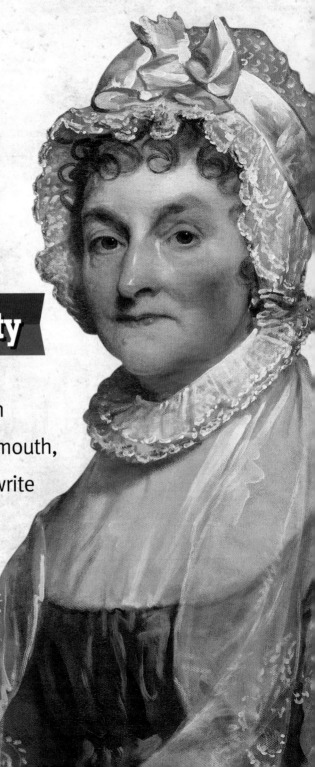

Abigail Adams

Voice of Equality

Abigail Adams was born on November 11, 1744, in Weymouth, Massachusetts. Taught to write and read at home, Abigail developed a passion for learning. She spent countless hours studying books.

Abigail married a lawyer named John Adams and settled into her new home in Braintree, Massachusetts. But her surroundings were anything but settled. Braintree was just outside Boston, where revolution stirred.

When John joined the Continental Congress, Abigail took charge of their home and farm. Women in the 1700s were not legally allowed to own property. But Adams referred to the land as hers and made wise investment choices.

Abigail and John enjoyed a loving and respectful relationship that did not suffer through distance.

They wrote to each other constantly.

She was his trusted adviser.

When the colonial troops needed ammunition, Abigail Adams melted the silverware in her home for bullets.

Besides being married to a president, Abigail Adams also raised one: her son John Quincy Adams.

Passionate for Rights

While John was at the Continental Congress, Abigail was already thinking about the new country's government. In a letter dated March 3, 1776, she urged John to "remember the ladies" in the new nation's laws. "Do not put such unlimited power into the hands of the husbands," she implored.

When the Declaration of Independence was written, Abigail Adams was upset to learn that the slave trade was not denounced in it. Adams was disgusted by slavery.

[Background: handwritten 1774 letter beginning "My Much Loved Friend ... Braintree october 16 1774 — I dare not express to you at 300 hundred miles distance how ardently I long for you..."]

History in the Letters

The letters revolutionary women wrote are primary sources that give insight into what they were thinking at that time. Abigail Grant, wife of a soldier who was cowardly in battle, taunted him in a letter: "come home & take care of our Children & I will be Glad to... take your place." Rachel Revere urged her husband, Paul, stranded after his famous midnight ride, to "keep up your spirits."

A 1774 letter from Abigail Adams to John. He was 300 miles away at the Continental Congress in Philadelphia, Pennsylvania. She remained home in Massachusetts taking care of their children and farm.

21

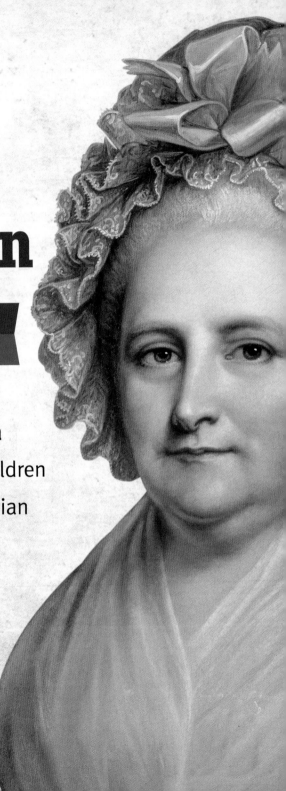

CHAPTER

4

Martha Washington

Fiercely Devoted

Martha Dandridge Custis was a
27-year-old widow with two children
when she married fellow Virginian
George Washington in 1759.

As revolution gripped the
colonies, George was chosen
to lead the **Continental Army**.
Beginning in 1775, he was

away from home for almost the entire war. Martha missed George and knew he needed her support. During the winters, when the army wasn't fighting, she braved hundreds of treacherous miles and weather, bumping about in a horse-drawn carriage through war-torn territory to reach wherever the army was encamped.

A Valuable Aide

Martha's arrival at camp boosted George's spirits and cheered the troops. She aided sick and wounded soldiers and made a large donation to buy clothing for the troops. Martha hosted foreign dignitaries, leaders of Native Nations and other officials at the encampment.

Tragedy and Triumph

While Martha was supporting her husband, her son Jacky worked as a delegate in Virginia's new state government. But Jacky wanted to be a part of the war effort, and he became an aide to George. In 1781, following the siege at Yorktown, Jacky contracted an infectious disease and died. Martha became one more of the thousands of brokenhearted mothers who lost their sons during the war.

Martha and George Washington celebrated Christmas Day in 1777 with the troops at Valley Forge, Pennsylvania.

Martha Washington was the first woman honored on a postage stamp, and the only woman on U.S. paper currency.

The third Martha Washington postage stamp (pictured) was issued in 1938. The first two appeared in 1902 and 1923.

After the war, Martha wanted to settle back at home with George. But the country had other plans. George was elected the first president of the United States. As Lady Washington, the country's first "first lady," Martha created customs and obligations other first ladies would follow. She carved her social role with dignity, always demonstrating her fierce devotion to the young United States.

The Edenton Tea Party

In 1774, one year after the Boston Tea Party, a group of women in North Carolina staged their own version of a protest against the unfair taxes England set on tea and clothing. Openly defying and protesting British laws was dangerous. These women risked arrest and imprisonment.

Taking Action

On October 25, 1774, 51 women in Edenton, North Carolina, drafted a declaration: they would boycott British tea and clothing until these products were no longer taxed by England. Legend says the women drank tea made from local herbs as they signed their names. The document stated that they could not stand by while the colonists' peace and happiness were affected.

The Edenton women reportedly drank tea made from mulberry leaves and lavender.

Bold Declaration

Penelope Barker, the group's organizer, sent a copy of the document to the British press, proudly revealing the women's identities. The men of the Boston Tea Party had not dared to reveal their identities—they even wore disguises.

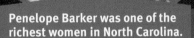

Penelope Barker was one of the richest women in North Carolina.

This bronze teapot weighs 250 pounds.

Pioneers

This was one of the first political protests by women, sparking more activism by women in other colonies. The Edenton women continued their boycott to nearly the end of the war. A bronze teapot sits atop an upright Revolutionary War cannon in Edenton in honor of these revolutionaries.

CHAPTER 5

Nanyehi / Nancy Ward

Beloved Woman and Cherokee Peacemaker

Nanyehi (Nancy Ward) was an Indigenous woman born in Chota, the Cherokee capital (now part of Tennessee), in 1738. At 17 she fought alongside her husband in wartime. During a battle between the Cherokee and the

Muscogee Creeks, another Native Nation, her husband was killed. Not to be defeated, she picked up his rifle and led the fight. For her bravery, she earned the title "Ghigau," or "Beloved Woman," and began voting on important tribal decisions. Later, as the leader of the Women's Council of Clan Representatives, she excelled as a **negotiator** and ambassador.

In a terrible time of war between the Indigenous people of North America and the encroaching American settlers, Nanyehi tried to achieve peace between them. When the American Revolution began, the Cherokee fought alongside the British to prevent losing more Cherokee land to settlers. Nanyehi didn't want increased hostilities between her nation and the American settlers, so she warned them before Cherokee attacks, saving many lives.

Generosity and Peace

As a Beloved Woman, Nanyehi had the authority to spare prisoners' lives. She saved colonist Lydia Russell Bean, a white woman captured during a Cherokee attack, from execution. The two shared their cultural knowledge, benefiting each other's communities.

In 1781, Nanyehi negotiated a treaty, allowing the patriot army to pass safely through Cherokee territory and win the war in Yorktown, Virginia.

The Confrontation by Cherokee Master Artist Talmadge Davis depicts Nanyehi saving captured colonist Lydia Russell Bean from execution.

The Indigenous Woman's Experience

As Europeans began to settle North America, Indigenous women wanted to maintain their people's sovereignty and keep their lands. They made choices they believed would protect their homeland by helping either the British or the colonists.

Degonwadonti (Two Against One), also known as Molly Brant, was a Mohawk woman who alerted British troops that colonists were about to attack them. She worked to persuade the Iroquois nations to keep fighting for the British.

Tyonajanegen (Two Kettles Together), an Oneida woman, fought for the patriots alongside her husband and son.

Tyonajanegen reloaded her wounded husband's gun and fired pistols for six hours in a battle with colonists.

Mary Ludwig Hays McCauley

Becoming a Legend

Women who displayed courage on the battlefield during the Revolutionary War are often known collectively by the nickname "Molly Pitcher." The story goes that a woman named Molly carried water to soldiers fighting against the British on the field during the Battle of Monmouth in Freehold, New Jersey, on June 28, 1778. Supposedly, when Molly's husband was wounded, she took his position at a cannon.

Mysterious Molly

But...who was Molly Pitcher? Many historians regard her as an unidentifiable legend, pieced together from the exploits of various women. In fact, many soldiers' wives were called Molly, a nickname for Mary, which was a popular name at the time. But one woman's documented actions match Molly's story best. Her name was Mary Ludwig Hays McCauley.

Mary Ludwig Hays McCauley was a soldier's wife who historians confirm was present at the Battle of Monmouth. The weather in Monmouth on the day of battle was brutally hot, and Hays was among the women carrying pitchers of water to the men who were fighting. Her soldier husband either collapsed from the heat or was wounded. When he was carried off the battlefield, she stayed behind.

Private Joseph Plumb Martin, a soldier at the battle, wrote down his account of a woman he observed loading a cannon: "a cannon shot from the enemy passed directly between her legs without doing any other damage than carrying away all the lower part of her petticoat." He added that she laughed off the close call and kept firing.

This Molly Pitcher statue stands above Mary Ludwig Hays McCauley's grave.

In 1822, the state of Pennsylvania, where Hays and her husband lived, recognized Hays's heroic efforts, paying her $40 annually until she died in 1832.

A memorial to Molly Pitcher was constructed near two springs that were used to supply water to soldiers on the battlefield during the Battle of Monmouth.

Deborah Sampson

Fighting in Disguise

Although women weren't legally allowed to fight in combat in the U.S. Armed Forces until 1977, one woman defied the conventions of the day and served on the battlefield 200 years earlier. Deborah Sampson was born in Plympton, Massachusetts, on December 17, 1760, to a poor family.

When she was 10, she became an indentured servant, working without pay in exchange for living in the home of a family in Middleborough, Massachusetts. It was not uncommon for children to work at the time. She probably cooked and cleaned. She educated herself by sharing the family's boys' schoolwork, and at 18 she became a teacher.

No one knows why Sampson decided to dress as a man and enlist in the Continental Army. But in May 1782, using the name "Robert Shurtliff," she made the decision to enlist in the Fourth Massachusetts Regiment.

Deborah Sampson was 5 feet 7 inches, taller than the average man, making it easy for her to disguise herself.

Margaret Cochran Corbin never fully recovered from the wounds she received during the Battle of Fort Washington, New York, on November 16, 1776.

Sampson was wounded during her first combat experience near Tarrytown, New York, on July 3, 1782. She removed the **musket ball** with a pocketknife and returned to duty.

In the summer of 1783, Deborah Sampson, still a soldier, was near death from a fever. Dr. Barnabas Binney, the doctor who treated her, discovered Deborah's disguise. Although he revealed her identity, she still received an honorary discharge and a **pension**, too.

More Women Warriors

Several other women are known to have fought in battles in the Revolutionary War. Here are a few of them.

★ **Margaret Cochran Corbin**, a nurse, took over her husband's cannon defending Fort Washington in Manhattan. She fired until she was severely wounded.

★ **Anna Maria Lane** dressed as a man to fight beside her husband. She was gravely wounded in the Battle of Germantown near Philadelphia.

★ Also disguised, **Sally St. Clair**, from South Carolina, was killed in the siege of Savannah in 1772. Only then was her gender discovered.

★ **Prudence Cummings Wright** formed a militia of 30 to 40 women in Pepperell, Massachusetts, in 1775 to protect the town while the men went to war.

Margaret Cochran Corbin joined 3,000 soldiers in a battle against 8,000 opposing troops.

More Founding Mothers Who Helped Shape the Nation

Esther de Berdt Reed (1746–1780)

Esther Reed led the Ladies Association of Philadelphia in 1780, raising more than $300,000 in the paper money of the time for the troops. She coauthored "The Sentiments of an American Woman," a publication that successfully appealed for women's war support by declaring women equal to men in patriotism.

Hannah Adams (1755–1831)

Born in Medfield, Massachusetts, on October 2, 1755, Hannah Adams became the first American woman to work professionally as a writer. Her first book was published in 1784, and her readers included John Adams (no relation) and other founders. Her proud father traveled around the country on a horse with copies of the book in the saddlebags, selling it door to door. Hannah Adams published four books in total, plus a short memoir.

Elizabeth Schuyler Hamilton (1757–1854)

Fascinated by political and military affairs, Elizabeth Hamilton became her husband's confidante and adviser. Alexander Hamilton was George Washington's aide, and Elizabeth spent time encamped with the troops during the Revolutionary War, along with Martha Washington. Once America was independent and Alexander served in Congress, she helped him develop ideas for the new American government. Later, she was a founder of the New York Orphan Asylum Society—New York's first private orphanage.

Dolley Madison (1768–1849)

As first lady to James Madison, who became the fourth president of the United States in 1809, Dolley Madison carried the torch of patriotism into the 19th century. Previously, she had assisted at dinners for widowed president Thomas Jefferson. She invited members of both political parties to her social functions in order to promote cooperation between the groups.

41

Mary Katherine Goddard (1738–1816)

Mary Goddard was a professional printer who published a revolutionary newspaper during the war. Congress asked her to print the Declaration of Independence, with all its signers included, for the public to see. In a bold declaration of her patriotism, she typeset her name as printer on the bottom. She is the only woman whose name is on a copy of the Declaration of Independence.

Timeline: Women and the American Revolution

Phillis Wheatley publishes her first poem in a Rhode Island newspaper. She is one of many women who support the revolution with their writing.

A group of 51 women stage the Edenton Tea Party to protest British taxes on tea and clothing.

1765 ▶ **1767** ▶ **1774**

Colonists upset about unfair taxes form the Sons of Liberty to challenge Britain's laws. Women patriots known as the Daughters of Liberty support the boycotts and begin production of goods like cloth, formerly purchased from Britain.

Anna Strong (1740–1812)

Historians suspect Anna Strong was a member of a spy ring that worked for George Washington. Operating across British-held New York and Long Island, the group's members gathered information for Washington and carried it across the Long Island Sound to patriot-held Connecticut. Strong was mentioned in one of the letters that passed between members of the ring, but, probably to protect her, she was never actually acknowledged as a member.

The Revolutionary War begins on April 19. Medical help is desperately needed for the patriot army. Many women work as untrained nurses and help wounded soldiers.

After the Treaty of Paris, the U.S. becomes an independent country. Women continue to fight for respect and equal rights.

1775

1783

The all-male Second Continental Congress meets in May. The wives of those men take responsibility for their families, homes, and farms, as did thousands of soldiers' wives when the war began.

Number of women in the Continental Congress: 0

Number of letters Abigail Adams exchanged with her husband during her life: More than 1,100

Number of months Martha Washington spent with the troops during the Revolutionary War: 52

Number of shirts made for the soldiers by the Ladies Association of Philadelphia: 2,200

Number of months Deborah Sampson served in the Continental Army disguised as a man: 17

Number of women who traveled with the Continental Army: About 2,000

Number of women who helped write the U.S. Constitution: 0

Did you find the truth?

F All Indigenous women sided with the British during the Revolutionary War.

T Women traveled to Revolutionary War soldiers' encampments to offer support and nursing care.

Resources

Further Reading

Greene, Carol. *Phillis Wheatley: First African-American Poet.* Chicago: Children's Press, 1995.

Lee, John, and Susan Lee. *Abigail Adams.* Chicago: Children's Press, 1977.

McGovern, Ann. *The Secret Soldier: The Story of Deborah Sampson.* New York: Scholastic Paperbacks, 1990.

Simon, Charnan. *Martha Dandridge Custis Washington, 1731–1802.* Chicago: Children's Press, 2000.

Woelfle, Gretchen. *Write On, Mercy! The Secret Life of Mercy Otis Warren.* Honesdale, PA: Calkins Creek, 2012.

Other Books in the Series

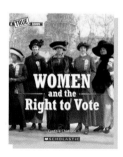
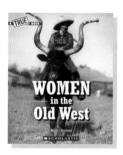
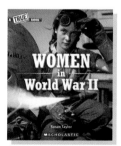

Glossary

abducted (ab-DUHKT-ed) taken away by force

colonies (KAH-luh-nees) groups of people who leave their home countries to settle in new areas

Continental Army (kahn-tuh-NEN-tul AHR-mee) the Revolutionary War army led by General George Washington

musket ball (MUHS-kit bawl) a round, lead object fired from a long gun called a musket before rifles and bullets were invented

negotiator (ni-GOH-shee-ay-tur) a person who tries to reach an agreement with others by discussing an issue or making a bargain

patriots (PAY-tree-uhts) people who love their country and are ready to defend it

pension (PEN-shuhn) a regular payment of money to a person who has retired from work or who cannot work because of a disability

politician (pah-li-TISH-uhn) a person who runs for or holds a government office, such as a senator

prejudice (PREJ-uh-dis) an opinion or a judgment formed unfairly or without knowing all the facts

sow (soh) to scatter seeds over the ground so that they will grow; to plant

Index

Page numbers in **bold** indicate illustrations.

About the Author

Selene Castrovilla's passion for the founding mothers was kindled by her discovery of the legendary life of a fellow native Long Islander, Anna Strong, who was said to have worked for George Washington's Culper Spy Ring. An acclaimed, award-winning author of four books on the Revolutionary War for young readers (and a forthcoming one on the Civil War), Selene has been a meticulous researcher of American history since 2003. A frequent speaker about the nation's beginnings, she is equally comfortable with audiences of children and adults. Please visit: selenecastrovilla.com.